and
Sticky

Written by Michaela Morgan
Illustrated by Andy Elkerton

Horribilly is a ...

BIG...

soggy...

green and gloopy...

monster.

He is the only monster at Golden Pond School.

One day his teacher said …

It's Sports Day today. Horribilly, you can be in a team with your friends.

Horribilly's friends were happy to have him in their team ...

but some of the other children were mean.

Horribilly is too slow and too sticky! Your team will never win!

Horribilly had a go at skipping …

but he had a bit of a problem.

Help!

So he had a go at running ...

but he was very slow and very sticky.

Horribilly sticks to the stick!

He was no good at throwing balls ...

or kicking balls.

He was no good at the three-legged race ...

or the sack race.

"I'm too big, I'm too slow and I'm too sticky," said Horribilly. "I'm no good at ANYTHING!"

"Cheer up, Horribilly!" said his friends. "You are not very good at skipping, running, throwing or kicking … but you are VERY good at being sticky."

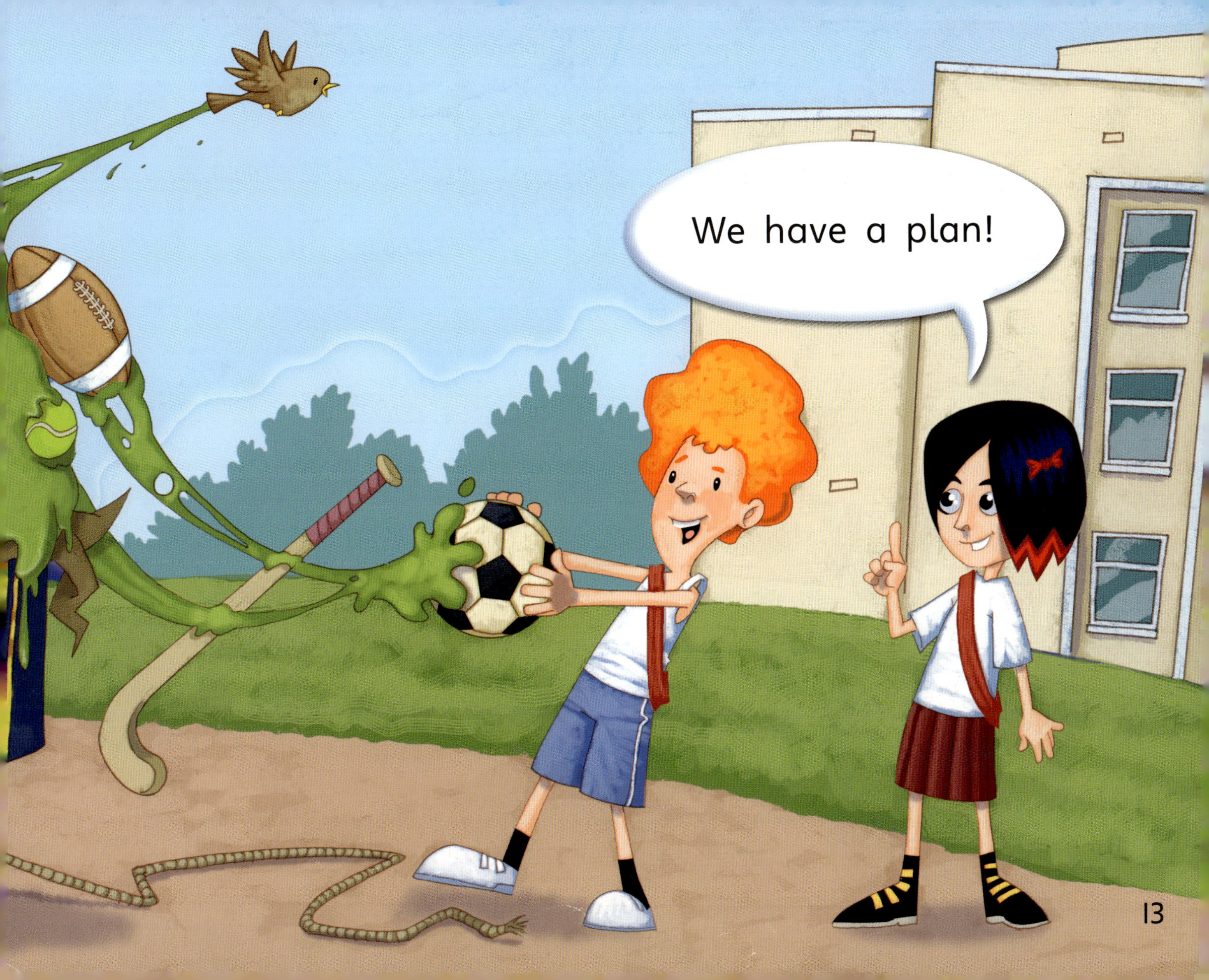
We have a plan!

Horribilly was very, very good at the egg and spoon race!

"Slow and sticky wins the race!" said Horribilly.